Aunty Uncle Poems
Gboyega Odubanjo

the poetry business

Published 2021 by
New Poets List
The Poetry Business
Campo House,
54 Campo Lane,
Sheffield S1 2EG

ISBN 978-1-912196-56-2
eBook ISBN 978-1-912196-57-9
Typeset by The Poetry Business
Printed by Biddles, Sheffield

Smith|Doorstop Books are a member of Inpress:
www.inpressbooks.co.uk

Distributed by NBN International, 1 Deltic Avenue,
Rooksley, Milton Keynes MK13 8LD

The Poetry Business gratefully acknowledges
the support of Arts Council England.

Supported using public funding by
ARTS COUNCIL
ENGLAND

Contents

i'm a young money millionaire / tougher than nigerian hair
– Lil Wayne

Sunday Service

okay let me say the words. let's see
what happens. we are rich because god
loves us. kills our enemies. i cannot wait to do up
nepotism. all my cronies drippy drippy.
god forbid i'm ever in church with nothing
to repent for. came with a plate. gonna leave
with food. want my blessing now. talk
to me about later later. i can feel it. listen:

okay close your eyes now. come together now.
who is with me here. said eyes closed.
don't worry it isn't anybody here but us. it's just
us. this is not a metaphor. this is the word.
the text. can hear it. there's someone. don't be
shy now. he isn't here. just us. just signal to the
ushers. they'll bring you. i know there's someone
in this room. ready to give. their body. an arm
even. just a touch. that's it. come forward.

World Parent

all the nigerian aunties and uncles are holidaying in dubai.
they're eating only nigerian food and talking only to their drivers.
they're posing as they give thanks, whatsapping everybody.
claim it's a kind of home that doesn't know their names
    so can't wish death.
say they like it because it holds no notions of them.
for example, all nigerians are liars who spin tales from imported fabrics.

*

it was a nigerian man who first discovered dubai.
the whole world in fact.
came descending with pockets full of sand and all manner
    of the earthly.
where there was water, took the sand, dashed it this way, that,
    and where it landed, stepped.
continued in this fashion so as to form plain, plateau, et cetera.
to everything he named and added names that no-one would ever say,
    liked the sound of his own voice.
prayed on land; his and of himself.
imagined it profitable.
dreamt of land black as oil and dark-skinned sons.
carved his name in tall letters everywhere, forgot how to spell it,
    improvised.
stepped back, looked at his work, This, and was large
    and proud.

*

seeing their son's work, his parents think, This?
    for why?
wonder if they bound him too much
    in freedom and comfort.
they think their son's hands spoiled;
    soft and pencil-friendly.
they think, instead of lawyer, doctor,
    This.
tell their friends of him,
    call him architect, do not say of what.

Fam

AUNTY 1 —gold tooth. kept the fanta fruit twists in her wardrobe. may she rest in peace.

UNCLE 1 —her husband.

COUSIN—the boy whose dad you went to for dry cleaning. your mum's best friend's younger brothers. the girl you used to hide with.

AUNTY 2 —the one who sits at the front in church. who has a bottle of baileys at weddings. wants it brought to her table in a black bag.

UNCLE 2 —always on old kent road. could get your sister and your actual cousin served at bars. always good for an alibi. played by the same actor playing COUSIN.

GRANDPA—there's books filled with pictures of him in the cabinet in the living room. the only man to ever make UNCLE 2 cry.

AUNTY 3 —first daughter of GRANDPA's second or third wife. never been the same since she came back from naij. elders say her mum had the same problems. to be replaced by a lighter-skinned actress during intermission.

NEPHEW—three years your senior. you will meet him today.

GRANDAD—when your dad jokes at the barbecue that you will drink anything he tempers it with the hope you don't become this man. you are yet to find a picture of him in the cabinet in the living room.

UNCLE 3—black sheep. elephant in this place. dark horse. dead horse. canned worm. pearled swine. anointed fly. scalped goat.

BIG MUMMY—your dad's stepsister. when you think of naij it is her face you think of. her marble floors and many servants.

In My Country

we can be a bit
boisterous says who
loud sure as the back
of a double decker
it's just our culture
a few things to know
bend your knees
when you greet don't ask
too many questions
it's left of the dealer
twos on jacks no jacks
on twos the queen's a slag
i don't make the rules
i just want to win it's not
that deep a man
talks about fucking another
man talks about mothers
it's not a party until they're
arguing about church
and we're cooking
our meat over burning
documents see i know a guy
he knows a guy
can get you whatever
a clean cup of piss mangoes
in november we got you
just need you
to pledge allegiance
to the singlet to the
oversized luggage

There Is Joy Breaking Here

and uncle is drunk already. uncle has his nephews
his special brew holding him up and happier
than the rest of us this bloodshot day of meat
and gisting. uncle grills burgers in knock-off birkenstocks.
plays coquet for aunty long since tired of his face
and fatuous self. uncle deep in meniscus. uncle cracks
the bone and swallows marrow. does not sweat or spill
a sip. uncle of independent means. clapping on the ones
and threes. jiving. got the old lady and the home office
and type 2 diabetes and maze and frankie beverly

                                        clapping on behind him

Diplomacy

Dad wants the head of the fish but Uncle is eyeing it up and in a better position to get it. Dad has just learned from Uncle's son that what Uncle really wants is a bigger portion of rice. Mind, we won't know if it really is Uncle's son for another two to four weeks but Dad, who can only assume it's Uncle's son, gives Aunty a look. Aunty, who is actually Cousin just much older, knows this look to mean if she can distract Uncle with what he really wants then Dad can get what he wants and he can give Aunty what it is she really wants, which is for her daughter to stop giggling with Uncle. This being another Uncle who, actually, isn't an Uncle at all. Dad knows that this Uncle would happily give up giggling with Aunty's daughter if someone could find him somewhere in the city that had good prices on necessities such as cow foot and ground crayfish. This Uncle's been here three weeks and, other than the food at this gathering, can't say he has tasted anything like what he is used to.

A Reminder to Mind Your Own

this table you're shaking.

this suede loafer you're stepping on.

this sofa arm you sit on in this shindig
we in every man deep bottles to hand
with the film over the carpet. the smell
of us. the dj swimming in the wet of us.
our arms a ceiling fan a rescue ship.
this worrying bass. plenty we're sorry
not sorry for. this place you pree. remember

       you don't have rights here. we don't
       know you from nowhere. you may know
       not what you do. you need to know here.

Tuesday

here we are fat
as husbands
a bag of peas
between us
i would change
the channel but
no one has paid
the bill and the man
coming to fit the box
needs me to phone
my guy who will
phone him and then
he'll call me back
i'm waiting the flies
in here like bailiffs
watching something
terrestrial and
from the buttocks
of my heart
what i wouldn't
for a cotch
to lay my hat
in east windows
that open all the way
an ice maker all
to myself
i wouldn't give
my name not laughter
but everything else

Dalston Lane

we huddle by the upstairs window   face the noise
  it is a street song kettled and screeching its own broken
yes

        we could watch it on the tv but do not trust
the definition of its bodies still learning to move to
this noise that scratches on them   skipping
so we look

              my dad is first to turn
he steps outside and squats on the roof of his car
throwing shiny objects onto the floor distracting
                              those who might approach him

my sister follows with a bucket
and a sponge   she washes the road of all its glass
and its blood   tells us that it is her glass and her blood
  refuses help

              my brother is stapling himself
to the street signs   my sister is washing his blood
which is her blood also   my brother has stretched himself
so wide around the noise and is checking everybody's papers
as they enter

              my mother stands on the corner of every road
in her arms is a book of names that she has given
and must give to the noise
  i stand behind her   holding her hand   waiting my turn
the noise is blurred big and still i am not knowing how to move

Butch Cassidy

because nobody is listening the colour palette here
is grey with condolence. the mayor tells everyone
that he is deeply saddened again. because nobody
is opening up the city reds itself. the realism is killing us.
we need cowboys. we need rugged individualism. o lord!

won't you give me an american death? because the reds
are that much brighter. we must make amends. we are done
with concrete. the sun is so lovely. before we die, let's count to five.

All I

After Martha Collins

always wanted a one black suit

wear it to my naming ceremony

funeral divorce party never need

to wash always fresh and black

picket stay off my lawn scallywag before i

all my neighbours jealous of my

benz daddy bought it cos i got into

school trouble boys will be big shot

bentley husband big booty wife

and yams bills on the table like it

when you say my family name no never

looked up what it means where from

goes back many many might be portuguese

Oil Music

call it a love song.
i'll get the bathtub ready.
  i'm in. we in ceramic.
let's say black. i'm bp
  you're shell. we all in.
we in the black. we both in
  a barrel. call it a village.
we both in the pumping. the people
  no get no nothing. no crabs in the river.
no periwinkles to pick. no day
  de pas where they no dey cry
suffer dis kind suffer like dis. we no care
  for them. i just want you to seep.
blacken my lot.

Home

After George Orwell

middle of the day when the van came   under the supervision of a pig

braying   quick   they're taking him   the animals broke off

            there   a large van

        lettering on its side   a man in a low-crowned

bowler hat sitting on the driver's

seat   the animals crowded round the van   good-bye

they chorused   good-bye   fools do you not see what is written

that van   he read   do you not understand what that means   the van

began to gather speed

and   at this moment   he heard the uproar   his face his nose

appeared at the window at the back of the van   the van gathering speed

        drawing away   there was

the sound   drumming of hoofs   inside the van

        the sound   drumming   grew fainter   died away

Blessed Princess Lady

my mother is a good english girl. she does not want. does not eat
for forty days until her father reveals her names in its dozens and
announces her a Lady. her parents are large, prominent members
of society. she marries young. on her wedding day she is a picture of
youth.

she gives her heart to a pot-bellied man who smokes cigars
and ashes on the carpet. she curses the women in his family. swallows
the tongues of the men and flowers their mouths.

when she finds
her heart it is a bouquet of chopped scotch bonnets. these my mother
cooks with plum tomatoes, onions, bell peppers, maggi and feeds to
her children who love her and hate propriety.

my mother dies
during a siege on her son's compound.

my mother is found dead
in her home. her body is displayed at westminster abbey. my mother
is a good christian girl.

my mother. full of grace. nothing be her body.
image alone. touch us spotless. pray for us.

it is the eighties and
my mother dances with john travolta, washes her hair, has picnics on
heritage sites.

my mother is a heritage site. my mother dies. dies again
in the biopics.

my mother is a white woman. nations weep. i am happy.
my mother is a white woman and is treated accordingly and this
makes me happy.

because it is the nineties my mother is hope, is holidaying in the south of france, is global.

my mother asks me to stop killing her. but i cannot i say. the work needs it and i am greedy for feeling. the tabloids need a story the people they need it i say.

every day we camp outside my mother's home watching her in the hours of her death. she comes to us with bowls of stew, tells us eat. thank you amen, we say.

Back to Sender

it's the third deliverance today
and i don't want to sound ungrateful
thank you for keeping your eyes closed
for me i told you i'm good but thank you for
the oil all on my forehead for the blessings but
i'm running out of space i'm in the market pushing
piety never worn intercepting all the prayers you sent
on my behalf what am i going to do with discernment when
i can't even remember which one of you lot owes me money wallahi
cor blimey no be me kill jesus no be me want forgiveness i swear pray
for the pagans save the myrrh and mercy for the opps cover london in
the blood

Saturday

it's only an hour 'til
last call and i want
to run there with you

on the news it's   no
                  don't go anywhere

and i'm law abiding
but also predisposed
several things
could happen here
i could tell you my story
you yours we could explore
the city say   hello mr officer
              we're just walking
              thank you
              good day to you also
and that would be that

the girl   her face in the posters
we might never have to learn
her name   everyone could make it
home before the papers are out
we could have a lovely time
tick all the boxes   phone all the numbers
charlie charles wouldn't pick up
he said he was getting out to pursue art
and he has   the guy your cousin
knows   who drives the merc
he says a drought's coming

i say   yeah bro
        our relationship
        with the ocean
        is unsustainable
he knows i know he meant
the streets and doesn't laugh
i don't mind   this is how tonight
is supposed to go

        your friends say i'm funny
        the streets flood the ocean
        floods   we know the names
        of all the girls they tell us
        themselves   we go every
        where and no-one stops
        us   my man picks up   we go

Babel

everybody going gone
people packed went
outskirts and elsewhere.
                    sound been bagged
                    aerial come down
              music plucked from sky
and scattered.
tower come down.
lives in matted
                    woven nylon zipped
                          uncle cousin
                    gone. bass in back-
packs. trunk rattle hushed.
couldn't no centre ever
hold all that racket, no.
                    woman on the 67 bus
                    with the stories
                          she's gone.
estate scrubbed clean
of its grimy self.
loiter song gagged.
                    gap-toothed whistle
                    no more. song not ever.
                    pastor on the corner
mistakes empty for heaven
communion run empty
no two or more gathered
                    no bodies here
                    only ghosts
                    and memory holding
this nothing
and nobody place up.

Grace

I am told that my grandfather liked to travel and that wherever he went he would write his name in big letters into the ground. Last week someone from New Jersey contacted me claiming that they had found his name written into one of their ports. There is a general agreement as to the amount of times my grandfather wrote his name into the ground, but nobody can be certain because there are too many ports. My grandfather had seven wives and my grandmother was, amongst other things, my grandfather's first wife. When I ask I am told that she, having failed to predict her own firstness, built herself into an anchorite made from her wedding gown and Yoruba words which all translate poorly. When I ask I am told that many of the words that would describe my grandmother translate poorly and so I am told that she was quiet and she died young quietly and that it just happened like that and that there is not really that much to be said about it.

Drake Equation

i'm running out of data on the train everyone is feeling particularly
    lonely it isn't enough
everyone & me ear plugged & stirring is listening to something
considering charts & cadence of feet bounce it is likely we are listening
    to drake

drake says sometimes i feel good sometimes i don't

he knows that until he bursts from carbs or cliché we will love him
always drake has been on our minds now for some fourhundredtwenty
weeks at least everyone & drake is wearing t-shirts with drake lyrics
printed on them we are signing love letters and suicide notes with
drakeisms it isn't enough wake up mumbling something drake drool
on our pillow wonder where else still we can find traces of him
    we're only now just learning

drake says more life more everything
    always more feeding every hour
    on the hour
    all the amenities
    the biggest residential pool
    on the planet
    everybody in it
    my critics & my friends
    fat happy house
    my children &
    everybody loving me
    the pictures
    portrait of the artist
    eating portrait

of the artist in
the biggest residential
pool on the planet
fat & happy
drake's ear is to the zeitgeist   listening for something out there
shooting his shot into space   waiting
it isn't enough
to hold everybody
& their faces   sing it
there are so many people
outside that haven't heard it
yet i don't know if
they can wait   how long
drake says   i do not know
what permanence is
i'm only now just learning
i'm upset   doing the best that i can
to be heard
i need more content

Shout Outs (Radio Edit)

this one's for all my.   in the whole wide.

    for requests it's.   i see you man.

      texts cost.   i always knew we were gonna.

  big up my girl tash wanna wish you a.   look at us.

  money good like.   make sure to get the bill payer's.

is good all the time and all the.   big up little derek doing.

remember we used to.   for times like.

  let's pour one out for.   rest in.   one time for the.

we don't die we just.   love from stokey.   totty in the.

    long life and.   everyone stay.

Brother

it's funny   because the world is
burning   this day is another

i wake up at 630   you south somewhere
wake up   the day is itself

metro become evening standard
become sleep   but today it's autumn

and it's been a court-mandated 12 months
so you're driving again   the world

is burning   i don't care   you say
you're going to buy a tesla and

we both know you won't   we won't
make a difference will we   easy listening

on repeat   'til it's smoke
in the car   smoke in the streets

Notes

'All I' is after '[white paper #28]' by Martha Collins.

'Home' is a found poem; the text is from George Orwell's *Animal Farm*, when Boxer is being taken away.

'Drake Equation' was inspired by the Canadian recording artist Aubrey Drake Graham and the American astronomer Frank Drake.

Acknowledgments

Thanks, always, to my family, friends, and teachers.

I am grateful to the following publications, where some of these poems (or versions of them) have appeared: *Bad Betty Press, MAP Magazine, Poetry London, SAND, SMOKE, wildness, The White Review.*